P9-DLZ-365

Life Cycle of a

Mushroom

Angela Royston

Heinemann Library
Chicago, Illinois

Published by Heinemann Library,
an imprint of Reed Educational & Professional Publishing,
100 N. LaSalle, Suite 1010
Chicago, IL 60602
Customer Service 888-454-2279

Designed by Celia Floyd
Illustrated by Alan Fraser
Printed in China by South China Printing Co. Ltd.

04 03 02 01 00
10 9 8 7 6 5 4 3 2 1

Library of Congress Cataloging-in-Publication Data
Royston, Angela.
    Life cycle of a mushroom / Angela Royston.
        p. cm.
    Includes bibliographical references (p.) and index.
    Summary: Introduces the life cycle of a mushroom, from formation of spores through underground growth of the mycelia to formation of mature mushrooms.
    ISBN 1-57572-210-0 (lib. bdg.)
        1. Mushrooms—Life cycles—Juvenile literature. [1. Mushrooms.] I. Title

QK617.R68 2000
579.6—dc21   99-046105

$13.95

Acknowledgments
The Publisher would like to thank the following for permission to reproduce photographs:

Ardea London/David Dixon, p. 21; Ardea London/D. W. Greenslade, p. 4; Bruce Coleman Collection/Hans Reinhard, p. 12; FLPA/A. J. Roberts, p. 25; FLPA/E. & D. Hosking, pp. 11, 18; FLPA/John Hawkins, p. 16; FLPA/Roger Wilmshurst, p. 20; Heather Angel, pp. 15, 23; NHPA, p. 13; NHPA/G. I. Bernard, p. 26; NHPA/Stephen Dalton, p. 8; Oxford Scientific Films/Barrie Watts, p. 9, Oxford Scientific Films/David M. Dennis, p. 19; Oxford Scientific Films/G. I. Bernard, pp. 5, 6, 10, 27; Oxford Scientific Films/Robin Redfern, p. 24; Tony Stone/Laurie Campbell, p. 14; Wildlife Matters, pp. 7, 17, 22.

Cover photograph: NHPA

Every effort has been made to contact copyright holders of any material reproduced in this book. Any omissions will be rectified in subsequent printings if notice is given to the Publisher.

Some words are shown in bold, **like this.** You can find out what they mean by looking in the glossary.

Contents

What Is a Mushroom?

A mushroom is a kind of **fungus**.
A fungus is like a plant, but it has
no green leaves. This fungus looks
like orange peel!

Spores

Threads

Growing underground

There are thousands of different kinds of fungi. This book is about a field mushroom, one of the few kinds of mushrooms that are safe to eat.

Button mushrooms

Ripe mushrooms

Years later

Spores

Like all kinds of **fungi**, mushrooms begin life as tiny **spores** in autumn. The spores grow on the underside of the parent mushroom.

Spores

Threads

Growing underground

Millions of spores blow away from the parent mushroom. Some of the spores land on the moist **soil** in this damp, grassy field.

Button mushrooms

Ripe mushrooms

Years later

Threads

A tiny **thread** grows out from the
spore. The thread grows longer
and longer. It branches into several
new threads as it grows.

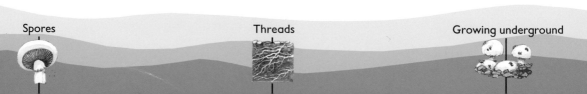

Spores   Threads   Growing underground

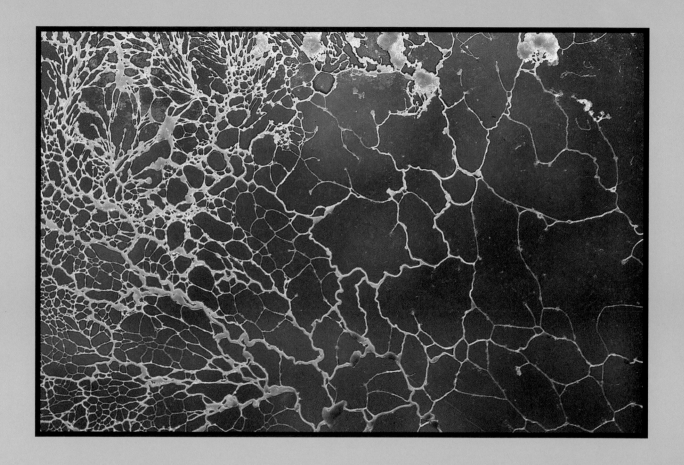

The threads take in food, water, and **nutrients** from the **soil**. Some of the threads join together with threads from other spores.

Button mushrooms

Ripe mushrooms

Years later

Growing Underground

It is now late summer. The **soil** is warm and damp. A small mushroom begins to grow underground on part of the web of **threads**.

Spores

Threads

Growing underground

Other mushrooms are growing,
too. They all live on the food and
water taken in by the threads.

Button mushrooms   Ripe mushrooms   Years later

Button Mushrooms

As the mushrooms grow bigger, the **stalks** push up through the **soil**. They are called button mushrooms because of their shape.

Spores

Threads

Growing underground

The mushroom's rounded top, or cap, opens up like an umbrella. There is a ring of thin skin where the cap was joined to the stalk.

Button mushrooms   Ripe mushrooms   Years later

Food for Animals

Some of the mushrooms are eaten by animals. Pigs eat mushrooms, and so does this hungry fox!

Spores

Threads

Growing underground

As the fox crosses the field, it smells the mushrooms. It chews up one or two of them.

Button mushrooms   Ripe mushrooms   Years later

Food for People

People like to eat mushrooms, too, but they must be careful. Never pick mushrooms you find growing **wild**, because they might be **poisonous**.

Spores

Threads

Growing underground

This woman is an **expert.** She knows which mushrooms are safe to pick and eat. She sells them to people.

Button mushrooms

Ripe mushrooms

Years later

New Spores

The underside of the mushroom cap has many thin ridges called **gills**. The gills of these ripe mushrooms are covered with millions of **spores**.

Spores

Threads

Growing underground

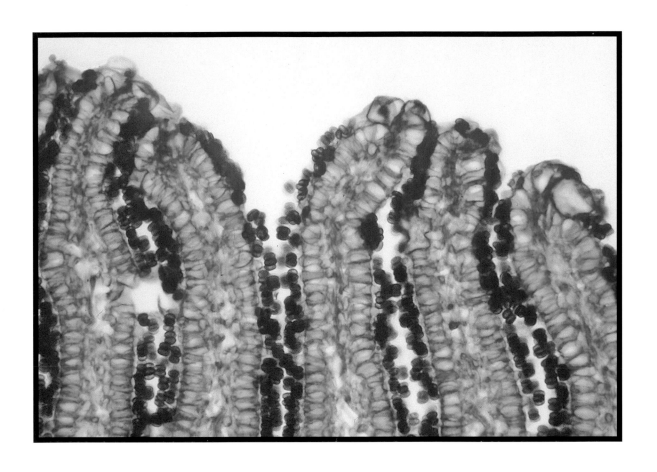

The spores are made inside special
cells along the tips of the gills.
After the spores are carried away
in the wind, the mushroom dies.

Button mushrooms

Ripe mushrooms

Years later

Spores on the Move

20

Sometimes the wind can blow the **spores** a long way. Some spores from the field mushroom ended up in this forest.

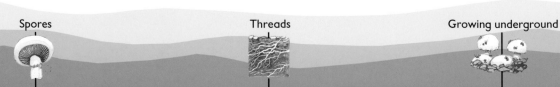

Spores   Threads   Growing underground

Many kinds of **fungi**, such as this honey fungus, grow in the forest. But the **soil** in the forest is not right for the field mushroom. Its spores will not grow there.

Button mushrooms   Ripe mushrooms   Years later

New Mushrooms

Some of the field mushroom **spores** fell in this wet, grassy field. They grew and made new mushrooms.

Spores

Threads

Growing underground

The **threads** in the old field grew some new mushrooms, too. In late summer, the new mushrooms pushed up through the ground.

Button mushrooms   Ripe mushrooms   Years later

Years Later

Every year, the underground **threads** grow to make new mushrooms. The mushrooms have spread out into a circle called a **fairy ring**.

Spores

Threads

Growing underground

A tractor is plowing up the field. As it breaks up the **soil**, the threads of all the **fungi** are destroyed. No more new mushrooms will grow.

Button mushrooms

Ripe mushrooms

Years later

A Mushroom Farm

Most of the mushrooms we eat are grown on special mushroom farms. Unlike plants, mushrooms do not need light to grow.

Spores

Threads

Growing underground

These mushrooms are growing in underground caves. It feels like autumn all year here, so new mushrooms grow all the time.

Button mushrooms

Ripe mushrooms

Years later

Life Cycle

Spores

1

Threads

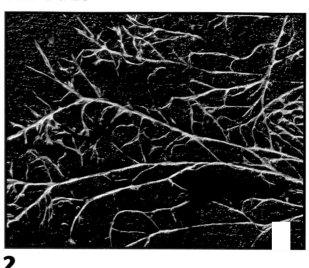

2

Growing underground

3

Button Mushrooms

4

28

Ripe mushrooms

5

Years later

6

29

Fact File

There are more than three thousand different kinds of mushrooms.

Each mushroom may make up to forty million **spores** every hour for about two days. Only a few of these spores will grow into new mushrooms.

A few kinds of mushrooms are so **poisonous** that they can kill you if you eat them, so do not pick **wild** mushrooms.

One kind of poisonous mushroom is called the jack-o'-lantern. It gets its name because it is orange, and it can glow in the dark!

Glossary

cells   tiny building blocks of living things

expert   person who knows much about something

fairy ring group of mushrooms that grow
   in a circle pattern

fungus   (more than one are called **fungi**) living
   thing that is like a plant but that does not have
   leaves

gills   ribbed underside of a mushroom

nutrients   chemicals that living things need to be
   healthy

poisonous   may cause sickness or death

soil   layer of dirt that covers much of the land

spores   tiny parts of a mushroom that can grow
   into new mushrooms

stalk   stem that joins a flower or fruit to the rest of
   the plant, or that joins the cap of a mushroom to
   its underground parts

thread   fine, hair-like group of underground
   mushroom parts that get food for the mushroom
   and help it stand up

wild   growing or living without the help of people

More Books to Read

Cooper, Jason. *Mushrooms*. Vero Beach, Fla.: Rourke Enterprises, 1991.

Fowler, Allan. *Good Mushrooms & Bad Toadstools*. Danbury, Conn.: Children's Press, 1998.

Murray, Peter. *Mushrooms*. Chanhassen, Minn.: The Child's World, 1995. An older reader can help you with this book.

Index